# *The Revelation of Bethlehem*

by

Two Hermits

One who prayed for One who wrote

Order this book online at www.trafford.com
or email orders@trafford.com

Most Trafford titles are also available at major online book retailers.



Printed in the United States of America.

*Imprimatur* +Timothy J. Harrington Bishop of Worcester July 17, 1985

The *Nihil Obstat* and *Imprimatur* are official declarations that a book is considered to be free of doctrinal and moral error. It is not implied that those who have granted the *Nihil Obstat* and *Imprimatur* necessarily agree with the contents, opinions or statements expressed.

Special Thanks to Marc Little who helped with the cover.
Original cover painting from unknown artist.
Nativity image inside the book from Dore.

Two Hermits (Writer), 1923 - 2001

The Revelation of Bethlehem.

Bibliography: p.
1. Bethlehem-Miscellanea. 2. Jesus Christ Nativity. I.
Title. DS110.B4T86 1985 220.6'4 85-8254 ISBN 0-932506-41-0

ISBN: 978-1-4669-0076-9 (sc)
ISBN: 978-1-4669-0077-6 (hc)
ISBN: 978-1-4669-0078-3 (e)

Library of Congress Control Number: 2011918504

*Trafford rev. 04/25/2012*

www.trafford.com

**North America & international**
toll-free: 1 888 232 4444 (USA & Canada)
phone: 250 383 6864 • fax: 812 355 4082

To

Hiroko Endo

a true sister

and

dear friend

with

love and gratitude

# Contents


I Bethlehem 7

The Grain Bin 10

II The Stable 15

The Grain Bin 18

III The Garden and The Field 23

The Grain Bin 27

IV Epilogue 49

Bibliography 52

# I

# BETHLEHEM

-I am by no means the least of all the cities in Judah; nevertheless, I am just a little town. I was once known as Ephrathah:[1] "the fruitful one," before my name was changed to Bethlehem: "the house of bread."

-Upon the two hills of my shoulders, twentyfive hundred feet above the level of the sea, my houses overlook the vine and olive-clad terraces that gradually slope down my sides. Past Rachel's tomb2 on my borders, and five miles to the northeast, is Jerusalem.

-Long ago the prophet Micah[3] prophesied that from me would come forth One who was to be ruler in Israel, and whose goings forth have been from of old, from everlasting.

-I had never understood why, of all places, it was to be from me that He would come forth, until the day it came to pass, and then I knew, because the heavens were opened to give me the answer.

-It was a night for watching, and never were the myriad stars brighter. Most of my children were fast asleep, but towards the south near Hebron and close to Migdal-Eder,[4] a few shepherds huddled near a fire keeping watch over their flock. They were men from Beth-Zur,[5] a small village not far from me, whose inhabitants were Calebites.

-While all things were in quiet silence, and that night was in the midst of her swift course, there was heard the cry of a newborn babe and the heavens above broke forth with loud shouts of joy. At that very moment I saw the gates of Paradise opening and heard someone call me by my old name: "Ephrathah." Before I had time to reply, I heard it again: "Ephrathah," and no sooner did I say: "Here I am," than I found myself inside a garden.

-Far below a young mother swaddled her infant, while two strong hands emptied grain from a manger into the hungry mouths of an ox and a donkey.

## The Grain Bin

*1. Ephrathah.* During the time of Jacob, and long before the twelve tribes took possession of the land of Canaan, Bethlehem was known by its old name: Ephrathah (Gn. 35:16, 19; 48:7). Even after the occupation of the Holy Land, the Bethlehemites acknowledged this in their blessing of Ruth, by making "Ephrathah" precede "Bethlehem" in their benediction (Ru. 4:11). The typical formula description of the ancient name of the town: "Ephrathah which is Bethlehem" (Gn. 35:19); "Ephrathah, the same is Bethlehem" (Gn. 48:7), finds echoes in the description of the original names of other towns: "Kirjath-Arba, the same is Hebron" (Gn. 23:2); "he called the name of the place Bethel, but the name of that city was called at first: Luz" (Gn. 28:19); "Jacob came to Luz which is, Bethel" (Gn. 35:6; Jos. 18:13; Jgs. 1:23, etc.). Changes in names are highly significant in Holy Scripture as in the case of Abram ("father of exaltation") to Abraham ("father of a multitude") and Jacob to Israel (Gn. 18:5; 32:28). The change in name from Ephrathah ("fruitful") to Bethlehem ("house of bread"), evokes not only the normal precedence of "fruit" before "bread," but also recalls for us the two stages of Mankind: Man in the fruitful garden of paradise, and Man in the field where he was taken from, and where in exile he learned to make, and eat bread. The two yearly harvest offerings to the temple also kept the uniform sequence, inasmuch as the early harvest offering was the *fruit* sheaf of barley called the *omer,* and the later wheat harvest offerings were the two freshly made leavened loaves of *bread* (Lev. 23:10-17).

2. *Rachel's Tomb.* Rachel died at childbirth just outside Ephrathah, which is Bethlehem in Judah (Gn. 35:16-19; 48:7). Jacob, her husband, buried her where she died and placed a memorial stone to mark her grave which the narrator in Genesis states was there even "unto this day" (Gn. 35:20). The tradition that the site of Rachel's grave was just outside Bethlehem is very ancient: "Rachel died there and was buried in the land of Ephrath, the same is Bethlehem, and Jacob built a pillar over the grave of Rachel on the road above her grave" (Book of Jubilees 32:34; 34:16; Testament of Joseph 20:3; Testament of Reuben 3:13; Targum Jonathan and Onkelos ad loc.; Flavius Josephus, Antiq. I. 21:3; Midrash Genesis Rabbah, Sec. 82.7-10; 97.1; Midrash Leviticus Rabbah 2.3; Pesikta Rabbati 3, IOb; Lekah Tob on Genesis 35:8, 20; Yashar Wa Yeshe 82b-86a; Book of Jasher 36:9-11;Beth ha Midrash,Vol.VI,pp.82-83, Edit. Jellinek; Rashi on Genes 48:7, etc.). Among the early Christian writers, Origen, Eusebius, and Jerome mention the same location. The site was visited, and the memorial stones commented on by the Pilgrim of Bordeaux (A.D. 333). Theodosius (A.D. 530), mentions that he saw there a "stone monument," as did Arculf (A.D. 670). Later on, in the twelfth century, Theodoric, Rabbi Benjamin of Tudela, and Moslem Idrisi also mention having seen Rachel's tomb just outside Bethlehem.

3. *Micah 5:2-4.*

4. *Migdal-Eder* ("Tower of the flock"). After the death of Rachel, Jacob with his flocks continued his journey towards Hebron and set camp in the vicinity of Migdal-Eder which is located about a mile south of Bethlehem. In this area "beyond the tower of Eder" (Gn. 35:21), occurred that incident with Bilhah, Jacob's concubine (v. 22), which cost Reuben his birthright, and set in motion the chain of events that resulted in Judah's preeminence from whom "came the chief ruler" (1 Chr. 5:1-2). The area in and around Bethlehem is very important in the history of Israel; for in the road by the fields a mile south of Ephrathah (i.e., Bethlehem), Benjamin was born (Gn. 35:16-19), from whom sprang Saul the first king of Israel and founder of the royal house of Benjamin (1 Sm. 9:1-2; 10:1, 24). And in Bethlehem itself, was born David the King and founder of the royal house of Judah. Also in Bethlehem was to be born the Messiah according to the prophet Micah (5:24), and Jewish tradition (Jer. Talmud, Berakoth 2:3, and Midrash Lamentations Rabbah 1.16). The area of Migdal-Eder, where Reuben lost the supremacy which was his by right of primogeniture, also plays a role in Jewish tradition concerning the Messiah, since it was to be there that King Messiah was to be revealed to Israel: "and Jacob proceeded and spread his tent beyond MigdalEder, the place where it is to be that King Messiah will be revealed at the end of days" (Targum Jonathan on Genesis 35:21). Thus, in the Gospel according to Luke (2:8), we are told that on the night the Savior was born "there were in the same countryside (near Bethlehem) shepherds abiding in the fields keeping watch over their flocks," and it was to them that the angel of the Lord revealed the birth of the Savior: "in the city of David" (Lk. 2:9-18).

Ancient Christian tradition has ever since reverenced the vicinity of Migdal-Eder as being the site where the angelic revelation was given to the shepherds. St. Jerome (c. A.D. 350), mentions that in his time the tower at Migdal-Eder was still extant: "about a thousand paces from Bethlehem is the tower of Eder which means 'tower of the flock,' a name which seems to be a prophetic allusion to the shepherds' future witness to the nativity of the Lord" (Onomastikon 43, 62, 68). We are told by Cyril of Scythopolis (A.D. 555) in his "Life of St. Euthymius," chapters 86 and 133, and the Pilgrim of Piacenza (A.D. 570, Edition Tobler at Molieniere, p. 107), that there was an ancient monastery there called the Poimenion (of the flock, in Greek); Arculf (A.D. 670), also visited MigdalEder and described it thus: "I have often visited the three tombs of the shepherds of the Nativity which are buried in the church near the tower of Gader, situated at about one thousand paces from Bethlehem" *(op. cit., p. 171).*

5. *Beth-Zur.* A small village close to Migdal-Eder and founded by Maon, a descendant of Caleb *(1* Chr. *2:42-45).* Holy Land pilgrims John Wormbser *(1591)* and Jean Boucher *(1610)* mention an old tradition that Beth-Zur was the "village of the shepherds" of the Nativity.

# II

# The Stable

-I am by no means the least of all His animals, but, let us face it, I am just a donkey. Not far from me is my companion, the ox, happily grinding away.

-From my stall I can see her whom I carried heavy with child over the hills into this crowded village. Do I have to say there was no room for them in the inn? That is why they are here.

-Why is it that I tremble yet feel a warmth and tenderness in my heart when I look at her? Can donkeys fall in love?

-He does things silently and well, the manger is clean and empty, he has filled it with straw and placed over it a small woolen mantle. He smiles at her, and I see her take the sleeping child and place him there, folding the coverlet over him.

-I must tell you about this town: "Bethlehem of Judah," known as the city of David the King, and seat of the royal house of Judah; the place the carpenter and his wife had to come to, all the way from Nazareth, to be enrolled in the decreed census· for they are of the royal lineage . . .

-We have a secret. "Of all the cities in Judah," why is it that "Bethlehem-Ephrathah" is not recorded in the list of cities belonging to the children of Judah? There is no mention of it in the scroll of Joshua,2 although everyone knows that it is indeed the city of the founder of the royal house of Judah, King David himself.

-My brother ox and I shall tell you why: it is because it was a city of Calebites,[3] a foreign people of the Edomitic Kenezite clan who incorporated themselves into the tribe of Judah, and from whom it is said that King David4 descended. It is all there in the grain bin.

-But I must be quiet now, for some shepherds have just come in bearing lambs upon their shoulders. Their eyes are full of wonder and Mary is showing them the swaddled babe in the manger.

-Outside the sheep are softly bleating, and I hear my companion give a deep sigh.

## The Grain Bin

*1. Census.* It was taken during the reign of Caesar Augustus (30 B.C.-A.D. 40), at the time when Cyrenius was rector and governor of Syria. His full name was Publius Sulpicius Quirinus (Tacitus, Annals 3:48). Cyrenius ruled twice in Syria, the first time unofficially between 3-1 B.C. (See Lapis Tiburtinus, Corpus Inscriptionum Latinarum, Vol. 14, p. 3613), and the second time as the appointed governor between A.D. 6-11 (Flavius Josephus, Antiq. 17.12.5; 18.1.1.2; 20.5.2; Jewish Wars 11:1).

*2. Joshua* 15:21-63. The list is quite complete, mentioning one hundred and twenty-five cities by name, and many of them smaller than Bethlehem, yet the city where the most illustrious member of the tribe of Judah was born, is not mentioned.

*3. Calebites.* The Calebites derived their name from "Caleb the son of Jephunneh the Kenezite" (Nm. 32:12; Jos. 14:6, 14), who was a descendant of Kenaz, son of Eliphaz, son of "Esau the Father of the Edomites" (Gn. 36:9-11). Kenaz was the founder of the clan called Kenezites, the foremost sons of whom were the same Caleb, and Othniel, his brother (Jos. 15:17; Jgs. 1:13; 1 Chr. 4:13). We first hear about Caleb in the narrative of the scouting done in the land of Canaan by the spies chosen by Moses from each of the twelve tribes (Nm. 13:1-33). It was at the same time the tribes were still sojourning in the wilderness with Moses and Aaron. They were then encamped in Kadesh-Barnea, an oasis in the desert of Paran close to the Promised Land. Moses assembled the tribes and selected from each one of them a delegate to spy out the land of Canaan and determine the strength of its inhabitants.

What wonderful names they had. From the tribe of Reuben, Shamua ("Renowned"); from Simeon, Shaphat ("Judge"); from Dan, Ammiel ("My people are strong"); from Naphtali, Nahsi ("Consolation"); from Gad, Geuel ("God of Salvation"); from Asher, Sethur ("Protected One"); from Issachar, Igal ("Deliverer"); from Zebulon, Gaddiel ("Fortune of God"); from Manasseh, Gaddi ("Lucky One"); from Ephraim, Hoshea ("Salvation"); from Benjamin, Palti ("Deliverance of the Lord"); but from Judah, Caleb ("Dog"). That Caleb (KLB) means "dog" is attested not only by the Hebrew meaning of the word (Jewish Encyclopedia Vol. III, p. 498), but by the same meaning for KLB in the Ugaritic texts: Keret 13.19; 5.10; 11 1.15; Baal V 3.60, in the Lachish Letters *(Tell El-Amarna) II* 4, and ancient Canaanite inscriptions *(Corpus Inscriptionum Semiticarum)*, Pt. 1.86; Pt. 11.56; III. 2225, Paris, 1881). Even in the Babylonian Tablets VAT 9933; 13836; 10349 (Berlin Museum), KLB means "dog." (See Young's Analytical Concordance.)

When the spies returned from their expeditions, almost all of them gave the people a discouraging report, frightening them with their accounts that told of great walled cities, high mountains, deep rivers, and gigantic inhabitants next to which they appeared to be mere grasshoppers in size. Only Caleb bravely spoke up saying: "Let us go up at once and possess it, for we are well able to overcome it" (Nm. 13:30).Along with Joshua, Caleb continued exhorting the frightened people: "The land which we passed through to search . . . is an exceedingly good land. If the Lord delights in us,then He will bring us into this land and give it to us, a land flowing with milk and honey. Only do not rebel against the Lord, nor fear the inhabitants of the land for they are bread for us. Their defense is departed from them, and the Lord is with us, fear them not" (Nm. 14:7-9). They spoke to no avail, and as the still badly demoralized people proceeded to stone them to silence, the Lord intervened, and rebuked and condemned the people and the rest of the spies except Joshua and Caleb - to wander in the wilderness for forty years until all of them who came out of Egypt had died. The Lord then spoke to Moses in praise of Caleb, saying: "But my servant Caleb, because he had another spirit with him and has followed Me fully, him will I bring into the land where he went and his children shall possess it" (Nm. 14:24).

Many years later, before the conquered land was to be divided by lot among the tribes, Caleb: the son of Jephunneh the Kenezite, went to Joshua to lay claim to his portion as promised by the Lord, and he was given first choice on any parcel of land he desired. And Caleb, who "wholly followed the Lord God of Israel" (Jos. 14:14), chose as his portion: Hebron, where all the patriarchs and matriarchs-save Joseph, Benjamin and Rachel-were buried. Seven times do the Holy Scriptures tell us that Caleb "wholly followed the Lord" (Nm. 14:24; 32:12; Dt. 1:36; Jos. 14:8, 9, 14; Sir. 46:10), as a dog follows his master (Tobit 11:4; Ahikar 2:85 Armenian text), and is proverbially faithful to him. Caleb obtained Hebron as his very own city and for a heritage to his descendants, so "that all the children of Israel might see that it is good to follow the Lord" (Sir. 46:10); and that they may discover that it was only fitting that a man named "dog" should ask, and get to keep the holy bones of his ancestors.

Bethlehem was founded by Salma, the grandson of another Calebite named Caleb (1 Chr. 2:51, 54, 9, 18, 19, 42, 50). And so Hebron and Bethlehem, which figures prominently in David's reign, were Calebite cities.

*4. King David.* Ancient rabbinic tradition traces the genealogy of King David from the marriage of Miriam, sister of Moses, to Caleb (Midrash Exodus Rabbah 1.17; Pirke Rabbi Eliezer 45; Targum on 1 Chronicles 2:19; 4:4; Sotah lib, 12 [Babylonian Talmud (BT)]; Sifre to Numbers 78; Midrash Tanchumah I. 52; II. 121-123 [edit. Buber]; Tan-wa-Yakhel, 4-5. See also Ginzberg's The Legend of the Jews, Vol. IV, pp. 81-82; Vol. II, 253).

The Rabbis may have surmised that King David was a member of the Calebite clan of Judah because he chose Hebron-the chief city of the Calebites-to be his place of residence, and seat of government during the seven and a half years he reigned over Judah (2 Sm. 2:1, 3, 11, 32; 1 Kgs. 2:11; 1 Chr. 29:27). It was also in Hebron that David was anointed King over all the tribes of Israel (2 Sm. 5:1, 3; 1 Chr. 11:1-3; 12:23, 28). King David himself may have acknowledged his Caleb (Dog) clan origins, by his choice of such selfdeprecatory expressions as: "After whom do you pursue? After a dead dog? After a flea?" (1 Sm. 24:14). And did not King David address himself as "son" to a Calebite? (1 Sm. 25:8, 2-3). That same Calebite was not only said to have been a "fool" (1 Sm. 25:25) but literally a "dog-man" (*anthropos kunikos* in the ancient Greek text of 1 Sm. 25:3), whose descendants King David, later on, threatened to exterminate as dogs (1 Sm. 25:22, 34 Literal Translation [Hebrew Text]).

# III

# The Garden

# and

# The Field

-I would have liked to say that it was a place of ineffable beauty, a fragrant garden of marvelous trees bearing fruits of every shape and color. And that a gentle breeze played upon the leaves while everywhere was heard the sound of rushing waters. I would have wanted to portray how upon the grass, the lion, ibex, and gazelle reposed, while in their midst lambs gamboled and otters frolicked in and out the streams.

-I longed to have told of a forest that rang with the singing of birds, and how the light danced upon their iridescent plumage. Yes, and even how the nectared flowers below hummed all in unison . . .

-But I only remember that it was a place for keeping, a garden place for Man.

-My eyes rejoiced in his glory for he wore as a garment the radiance of the sun, and the ground beneath him shuddered with pride. It was he who called my name and beckoned me towards him.

-He was standing by the tree of life in the middle of the garden, and though I saw eternal knowledge in his eyes, it was the strength of his understanding that drew me to him.

-Ephrathah, my fruitful one, mother and shelter of the children of men. Come, and I shall tell you what labor and sorrow have taught me. Many eons ago in the womb of time, the Lord Elohim took and formed me from the dust of a field which had been moistened by a mist from the ground. And making me into His own image and likeness, He breathed into my nostrils the breath of life.

-Now I understand, why He took me from the field where I was formed and brought me into this watered garden: it was to place upon me the seed of His command,] and wait for me to bring forth fruit from it.

-I accepted, and kept the seed of His word, but when I reached out to partake what was forbidden to me, I cast that seed aside, and consumed what I had not yet brought forth for Him: fruit from the seed of His word.

-I knew then, that to choose fruit and reject seed, is to choose the end of all growing. And where there is no growth, there is death.

-The Lord Elohim exiled me back to the field where I was formed, there to bring forth in labor and sorrow what obedience in a garden would have gained for me.

-Come, my Bethlehem, let me take you by the hand to the place of understanding, said the Man. And he led me outside the gates of Paradise into a field of grain.

-Here, he said, in this field where I was taken from, is where I plowed, harrowed, sowed, and tilled. And here is where I learned to understand, that from the sweat of my labor was the dry earth to be watered, and by my strength its furrows to be made.

-Many a time did I press my face in tears upon it, for though I sowed good seed, there sprang forth thorns and thistles to grieve my heart and pierce my hands.

-And thus in sorrow did the first green blade appear, and then the ear, and after that the full grained fruit that waves before you, golden in the sun.

-These children seeds, the offspring of my labor, whom I must reap before I shall gather them into my arms.

-Then shall these "sons of my threshing"3 be brayed and ground by my Eve, who shall knead and press them to the leavened form that fire shall make into the Bread of Man.[4]

## The Grain Bin

**1. Seed of His Command.** When we are told in the book of Genesis, that the Lord God created Man in His own image and likeness, and formed him from the moistened dust of the ground, we are given the basis of understanding the nature of Man, his origin and end. Man is truly an Earthman, and he shall return to the earth at the end of his days: "the Lord created Man of the earth and turned him into it again" (Sir. 17:1; Gn. 2:7; 3:19). Since "Adam was created of earth" (Sir. 33:10), all his progeny are "offspring of him who was first made of the earth" (Wis. 7:1), and back to the earth they shall also return (Job 10:9; 33:6; 4:9; Eccl. 3:20; 12:7; Is. 45:9; 64:8). "What then is Man but he that is only earth and potter's clay and will return to dust?" (I Q H 10:3-4; I Q S 11:22; Dead Sea Scrolls).

In creating Man from "dust," God made him from topsoil, that "highest part of the dust of the world" (Prv. 8:26) which is potentially the most fertile portion of the ground, pending a good supply of water. Man was formed of earth and water: "a mist went up from the earth and watered the whole face of the ground, then the Lord God formed Man of dust from the ground"(Gn. 2:6). Previous to that, the rest of the ground was not yet productive, "for the Lord God had not caused it to rain upon the earth" (Gn. 2:5). "The dust of the earth can be blessed only through water" (Midrash Genesis Rabbah 41.9).

Having formed Man from the moistened dust of a field, the Lord God brought him to a fruitful Garden, a superlative place for growth and production, where the soil was best and there was a plentiful water supply (Gn. 2:8-15). There was no better spot to bring a living plot of potentially fertile earth into, should one have wished to sow upon it and obtain fruit in abundance. It was after He had brought man into the garden that "the Lord God commanded (vaytzav) upon (al) the man" (ha-adam) not to eat the fruit of the tree of the knowledge of good and evil (Gn. 2:16-17). It is literally written that the Lord God commanded "upon" Adam as one would place a "seed . . . upon (al) the earth" (Gn. 1:11), and wait to have it accepted, kept and brought into fruit. It is the nature of good ground to bear fruit from seed, and to nurture what has sprung forth from it. In doing so, the seed is, as it were, brought to perfection and multiplied in the fruit, to the benefit of the sower and the commendation of the soil.

Upon the great truth that Man is literally an "earth"-man formed from the dust of the ground (Gn. 2:7; 3:19; 28:14; job 19:9; 34:15; Eccl. 3:20; *12:7),* rests all our understanding as to his nature and potential. Thus Man's relationship with his Maker is basically that between earth and Sower, garden and Gardener, ground and Seed, matter and Life. That is why the Word of God is often described as a seed implanted in man: "As . . . seed to the sower . . . so shall My word be that goes forth out of My mouth" (Is. 55:10, 11). "The Seed is the Word of God" (Lk. 8:11). "The Sower sows the Word" (Mk. 4:14). "Receive with meekness the implanted Word which is able to save your souls" (Jas. 1:21). "Born again not of perishable seed but of imperishable: through the Word of God which lives and abides forever" (1 Pt. 1:23). Philo, a Jewish philosopher (20 B.C.-A.D. 42), described the Word of God being "the invisible seminal artificer: the Divine Word" (Philo, Quis, Rer. Div. Her. 67) and as such it is the vitalizer through which God effects His will in Man and also gives life to him, because seed is the original starting point of life in living creatures.

A plot of earth in a garden is most productive when it bears a fruit tree. When "the Lord God took the Man, and put him into the Garden of Eden to work it and to keep it" (Gn. 2:15), He brought him to a place full of fruit trees which the Lord had made to grow out of the ground (Gn. 2:8-9). Man was brought there to take care of the Lord's own garden, but as earthman he had, in a certain way himself, the capability to bring forth a fruit tree from seed sown upon him. In other words, Man could have been himself not only the garden of the Lord but the fruit-bearing tree in it, had he kept the seed of God's command, "the Paradise of the Lord, the Trees of life, these are His holy ones, their planting is rooted forever, they shall not be uprooted" (Pss. of Solomon 14:3-4; 1 Q H 8:5, 6, Dead Sea Scrolls). "What blessings God bestows on those who love Him as they should since they become a paradise of delights, they rear in themselves a fruitful tree in fullest bloom and are adorned with a variety of fruit" (Epistle to Diognetus 12:1-2).

Unfortunately, in discarding the seed of God's command, and devouring the forbidden fruit, Adam cast away life, and consumed in the ripe fruit the dissolution that follows end of growth: death. For "growth is effected by seed" (Philo, Leg. Alleg. II.37) and not by fruit substance. There is life in seed, a life that endlessly engenders itself in the ground that holds the seed fast, and nurtures it. Let us never forget that when the good ground keeps the seed, it awakens life in it. In keeping the Seed of God's Word, Man would have learned that the utility or service of good earth is to keep seeds and awaken life in them towards growth, and the bringing forth of fruit full of children seeds. As an ancient writer comments of the Lord: "I, the Lord knew his (Adam's) nature but he did not know his nature" (Secrets of Enoch 30:16), because he did not keep the seed which would have produced in him "the fruit of knowledge." "The fruit of whose knowledge is upon his body" (Sir. 37:22 Hebrew text), is he who has kept the commandment entrusted to him as a seed, towards the "bearing fruit . . . and increasing in the knowledge of God" (Col. 1:10) expected of him.

From the narrative of the Fall of Man, found in the book of Genesis (3:1-24), we learn that it is by keeping the Seed of His command that we shall receive the fruit of knowledge. As the Lord said: "If any man does His will, he shall know . . ." (Jn. 7:17), "they have kept Thy word, now they know . . ." (Jn. 17:6, 7). For in doing His will we gain His friendship and thereby His knowledge, because friends confide in one another (Jn. 15:10, 14-15). The wise scribes knew that the prohibition given to Adam by the Lord God was indeed a commandment whose keeping would result in "knowing": I ordained that he (Adam) should observe the decree and keep the commandment. (Secrets of Enoch 31:1)

> Thou (Adam) hast forsaken My commandment which I delivered unto thee to keep it. (Book of Adam and Eve 23:3)
>
> You commanded upon him (Adam) just one commandment that he may know . . . (4 Ezra 3:7, Armenian text)
>
> Is not the keeper . . . He who knows? (Prv. 24:12)
>
> If they obey not . . . they shall die without knowledge. (Job 36:12)

It is because the Word of God is given to us in the form of a seed that a wonderful thing happens in the heart of those who hold it fastthe Seed opens up in them: "the opening (pethach) of Thy words gives light causing the simple to understand" (Ps. 119:130, Literal translation). The Seed of the Word of God opens up in the hearts of the simple because "the simple believe every word" (Prv. 14:15), they hold fast what is given them to keep. There is "light" within the Seed of His Word, and because the righteous also believe and hold fast to the Words of God, it may be truly said that "light is sown (zara) for the righteous" (Ps. 97:11). This "light" within the Seed of His Word, is the "light of knowledge" (Hos. 10:12 Greek text; Testament of Levi 4:3; Testament of Benjamin 11:2), for God "sends knowledge as the light" (Sir. 24:37, Latin Vulgate [LVI) because we must have light to "see and know" (Is. 8:20; Jer. 5:1). "The light of the knowledge of the glory of God" (2 Cor. 4:6) that is hidden in the Seed of His Word, becomes manifest, in "the fruit of light" (phos) which the righteous will bring forth from the good ground of their hearts. That is why it is written that "the fruit of light (phos) is in all goodness and righteousness and truth" (Eph. 5:9).

Though lowly and small in size, there is great potential stored within a seed. The garden ground that accepts the seed, in reality accepts the fruitful tree that shall spring forth from it. They who accept the Word and cooperate with it shall bring forth knowledge and understanding. "Hear the (seed) Word of Truth and receive the knowledge and understanding of the Most High" as fruit from it (Odes of Solomon 8:8). "If you remain in my Word . . . you will know the truth" (Jn. 8:31, 32). They who shall bring forth the fruit of knowledge by keeping the Seed of His command, shall not only receive the knowledge of God but life everlasting as well (Jn.17:3), because there is life in all seeds. From that Seed "word of Life" (Lk. 8:11; Phil. 2:16; 1 Jn. 1:1), shall spring forth a "tree of life" (Gn. 2:9; Rev. 2:7; 22:14) in those who hold it fast. Truly, "Wisdom is a tree of life (in the end) to those who take hold of her" as a seed in the beginning (Prv. 3:18). Thus we are told: "Keep my commandments and live" (Prv. 4:4; Lev. 8:5), for the Seed of "His commandment is life everlasting" (Jn. 12:50). "If you will enter into life, keep the commandments" (Mt. 19:17). "Blessed are those who do His commandments so that they may have a right to the tree of life" (Rev. 22:14) for "the tree of life is for all those who do his will" (4 Mc. 18:16). They who do His will are they who please Him (Jn. 8:28, 29), and "they that do the things that please Him shall receive the fruit of the tree of immortality" (Sir. 19:19). The excellence of knowledge is that it "gives life to those who have it" (Eccl. 7:12) provided that the knowledge they have is the knowledge of God and His good things.

There is "salvation for all those who obey Him" (Heb. 5:9), for "Life is in His will" (Ps. 30:5 Greek text), but "if they obey not they shall perish . . . and they shall die without knowledge" (Job 36:12). They who cast away the Seed of His command cast away life and knowledge of God. And they who disobediently seek to know evil seek death because just as "life and good" go hand in hand, so do "death and evil" (Dt. 30:15). Therefore "He that keeps the commandment shall not know any evil thing" (Eccl. 8:5), for to know evil is to die. They who accept the "evil seed" (4 Ezr. 4:30, 31) sown by the "evil one" (Mt. 13:19, 38), "bring forth fruit unto death" (Rm. 7:5), but "if anyone keeps My Word, he will never see death" (Jn. 8:51) said the Lord, for His "Words . . . are spirit and life" (Jn. 6:63), they are "Words of eternal life" (Jn. 6:68) for those who keep them. When David cried out: "I will set no wicked thing before my eyes . . . I will not know evil" (Ps. 101:3, 4), it is because David knew that "the knowledge of evil is not wisdom" (Sir. 19:22) but death. Nehemiah was wise when he wrote: "I come to Jerusalem and understood (bin) of the evil that Eliashib did for Tobiah" (Neh. 13:7). He did not write "knew of the evil" but used the word "understood," because he knew "to depart from evil is understanding" (Job 28:28), but to know evil is to die (Gn. 2:17; 3:4-7,17-19). For when we "know" something we make that which we know part of ourselves, we incorporate knowledge. The knowledge of evil is death but the knowledge of the "good seed" (Mt. 13:24) of the "Word of life" is life everlasting (Phil. 2:16; 1 Jn. 1:1; Jn. 17:3; 1 Jn. 5:11-12). Thus the book of Proverbs tells us that just "as righteousness leads to life so he who pursues evil pursues it to his own death" (11:19).

"What can be known about God is plain" (Rm. 1:19), if we look at His creation with the eyes of wonder and the heart of a child. For "ever since the creation of the world, His invisible nature, namely, His eternal power and deity, has been clearly perceived in the things that have been made" (Rm. 1:20). If Earthman is to be "exalted . . . out of the dust" (1 Kgs. 16:1) it must be through the keeping of the Seed of God's Word. For just as the lifeless elements of the ground are taken up to form part of a living tree through the initial keeping of the seed of that tree by the ground, so is Earthman to be raised up to life everlasting by his keeping of the Seed-"Words of eternal life" (Jn. 6:68).

Only through the keeping of a living seed may the earth aspire to life in the living tree sprung forth from it. And because God is infinitely wise, only by being kept and nurtured will life awaken in that seed, and the seed be multiplied by the earth that kept it. From one seed shall spring forth many seeds if the original seed is held fast and nurtured by the ground. God's first command to Earthman was to "be fruitful and multiply" (Gn. 1:28) but Man had to learn that there is no fruition or multiplication unless the seed is kept. In devouring the fruit, Man disobeyed and did not keep the Seed of God's command, he thereby forfeited the life and knowledge of God found within the Seed of His word. To "have life . . . more abundantly" (Jn. 10:10), we must keep the Seed-"Word of life" (Phil. 2:16; 1 Jn. 1:1; Jn. 6:63, 68; 12:50), and "knowledge shall be increased" (Dn. 12:4), if we first "keep knowledge" (Mal. 2:7; Prv. 5:2; 10:14) as a seed in the ground of our hearts. The earth that holds fast to the seed shall exalt it in the fruit-bearing tree brought forth from it. Man was created to give glory to God, and because he was formed from the dust of the ground, man gives glory to God the same way the ground may be said to give glory to the sower: by bringing forth fruits in abundance from the *seeds* sown by him. "In this is My Father glorified, in that you bear much fruit" (Jn. 15:8). Only the ground that is "good" shall bear much fruit (Mt. 13:8, 23; Mk. 4:8, 20; Lk. 8:8, 15), therefore the fruits are known as "the fruits of righteousness" (Phil. 1:11; Heb. 12:11; Rm. 6:22). "Honor the Lord with thy just labors and give Him the first of thy fruits of righteousness" (Prv.

3:9 Greek text). We give glory to someone when we praise that person, therefore "praise to God . . is the fruit" (Heb. 13:15) brought forth by the righteous who hold fast the Seed of His word (Ps. 1:1-3; Jer. 17:7-8); "praise . . .the first-fruit of the lips from a holy and righteous heart" (Pss. of Solomon 15:5). The good are the "Trees of righteousness, the planting of the Lord that He might be glorified" (Is. 61:3) by the "praise" found in their "fruits of righteousness." It is for this "precious fruit of the ground" that the Lord "waits for" with "long patience" (Jas. 5:7).

"Blessed are all they who accept the words of Wisdom and understand them" (Enoch 99:10); because they have accepted and kept them as seeds. For he who "receives the seeds of Wisdom" (Philo, Q. Gen. 111.32) and keeps them, shall bring forth "the fruits of Understanding" (Sir. 37:22) to the exaltation of Wisdom (Sir. 24:13, 14). Truly "Wisdom is justified by her children"-seeds (Mt. 11:19). Thus "God sowed understanding in earthborn man" (Phil. Leg. All. 1.79) when He gave him His word to keep so that man would make it manifest in "the fruits of his understanding" (Sir. 37:23), to the glory of God.

From the Holy Scriptures we learn that Man is not only "dust" (Gn. 3:14)-the residue of the earth-but also "ashes" (Gn. 18:27; job 30:19; 42:6; Wis. 2:3; 15:10; Sir. 10:9; 17:32; 40:3), the residue of firewood. Because Earthman was meant to become a Treeman bearing the fruit of life and knowledge, and providing shelter and light as well. If the Lord God gave Earthman a Seed to keep in the beginning, it was so that He would receive fruit from him as a Treeman in the end. And all this was to be accomplished by the keeping of the Seed of God's command, for it is through a living seed that matter enters into life. That is why Man is not only called Adam from the Hebrew word for "ground": adamah, but he is also called ish (another Hebrew word for "Man") from the Hebrew word "fire": esh. Thus when the Lord opened up "the eyes of 'his' understanding" (Eph. 1:18; 1 Jn. 5:20; Lk. 24:45) the blind man cried out: "I see men as trees walking" (Mk. 8:24), because along with sight and insight: "the Lord gives Wisdom to the blind" (Ps. 146:8 Greek text).

**2. Field.** Both the ground of a garden and that of a field bring forth fruit from seed, but the ground of "a most fruitful garden" (Sir. 40:17) does so almost effortlessly for a "garden causes the things that are sown in it to spring forth" (Is. 61:11), but afield must be cultivated before it can produce. One goes to a field for labor and to a garden for pleasure.

When the Lord created all living things He made them perfect, and ready to be able to procreate themselves perfect and complete through their seeds. "In the original creation of all things . . . God caused all the trees and plants plants to spring out of the earth perfect, having fruits not unripe but at their prime . . . also a provision for the perpetual reproduction of their kind containing within them seed" (Philo, De Opif. 42, 43). "All creatures were created in their full stature . . . the trees laden with fruit" (Rosh Hashanah lla, b; Hulin 60a, [BT]; Pirke de R. Nathan 5; Midrash Konen 25; Haggadah Bereshith 23; Torah Shelemah 1.582, 592). "All issued forthright complete and perfect out of the earth . . . the fruit was created first" (Midrash Hagadol Bereshith 1.581; Torah Behukothai 1.561; Torah Shelemah 1.384, 389; Midrash Talpiyot 5704). "Like all creatures formed in the six days of creation, Adam came forth from the hand of the Creator fully and completely developed" (Hulin 60a; Hagigah 12a, [BT]; Midrash Genesis Rabbah 14.7; 8.1; Midrash Bamidbar Rabbah 12.8; Midrash Song of Songs Rabbah 3.11; Sifra 26.4; Zohar 1.123b; Philo, De Opif. Mund. 13, 47, 140, 145; St. Jerome, Q. Heb. in Gen. 1.902; St. Ephrem, Op. Omn. I. 59). Ancient tradition also mentions that although the trees were created laden with fruit containing seed after their own kind (Gn. 1:11-12) it was "not yet in their power to engender fruit" (Hulin 60b, [BT]; Midrash Haneelam 13b) "for the Lord God had not caused it to rain upon the earth and there was no man to work the ground" (Gn. 2:5). It was as if the Lord God delayed the propagation of all plants and trees until Man was created and formed from the moistened dust so that Man might see that all new growth and fruit-bearing issues from seeds that are kept and acted upon by the good ground which has the perfect pattern before it.

Because of its protected environment, rich soil and good supply of water, a garden is like a nursery seed plot: an ideal place for the germination of seeds. The Garden of Eden would have also been an ideal place for Man to have acquired the knowledge of God, because it was a perfect place for friends to meet and get to know one another. Simple knowledge may be gained by sight or by touch, but "the knowledge of God" (Hos. 6:6; Is. 11:9; Hab. 2:14) is "eternal knowledge" (I Q S 2:3; 8:9; I Q M 17:8, Dead Sea Scrolls) which the Lord gives only to those who obey Him and keep the Seed of His command. "God loves knowledge" (Zadokite Frag. 2:3) and He desires us to have His knowledge, because we go from the knowledge of God to the love of the Lord. The Lord said: "I desired . . . the knowledge of God . . . but they like Adam have transgressed the covenant, they have dealt treacherously against Me" (Hos. 6:6, 7). They transgressed and forgot that the knowledge of God is based on a faithful personal relationship with Him, a knowledge that increases in us as we become aware of His thoughts, manner, and Person through our keeping of His ways: "Make me to know Thy ways that I may know Thee" (Ex. 33:13). The ways of God are made known to us through the Seed of His word, hence it is "the words of the Law which direct a man's understanding to the knowledge of the All Present One" (Midrash Numbers Rabbah 14.4).

"The Word of God is alive" (Heb. 4:12 Literal translation) and is "His Seed" (Lk. 8:5, 11), and because it is the Seed of God (1 Jn. 3:9) it carries within it the promise of immortality and eternal knowledge. Truly, the Word of "His commandment is life everlasting" (Jn. 12:50) to those who hold it fast. Whosoever keeps "the word of life" (1 Jn. 1:1; Jn. 6:63, 68; Phil. 2:16) keeps life (Prv. 3:1, 2), and "keeps knowledge" (Prv. 5:2; 10:14; 12:23; Mal. 2:7) as well. For we must not forget that life and knowledge are in the Seed of God for the sake of the potential "son" within that seed: the inherent child of God hidden inside the Seed of His Word, waiting to be brought forth by the matrix ground of our hearts. The "Son" is in the Word of life as the very germ of it: "Who has the Son has life and who has not the Son of God has not life" (1 Jn. 5:12). To those who "received Him (as Word-seed in their hearts), He gave power to become children of God" (Jn. 1:12, 1). Giving them power to be "born again not of perishable seed but of imperishable, through the Word of God which lives and abides forever" (1 Pt. 1:23). Thus, he who keeps the Seed of His Word shall "grow in grace and in knowledge of our Lord" (2 Pt. 3:18), becoming "fruitful in every good work and increasing in the knowledge of God" (Col.

1:10; Phil. 1:9) until he shall "attain to . . . the knowledge of the Son of God, unto a perfect (teleion) man" (Eph. 4:13), "renewed in knowledge after the Image of Him who created him" (Col. 3:10). On the other hand, those who cast aside the living seed of His command, cast away life everlasting, and became barren and "unfruitful in the knowledge of our Lord" (2 Pt. 1:8).

When field-ground that is transferred to a well watered garden does not produce in the optimal place for fruition, it is taken back to the field where it came from. And there, it is plowed, sowed, harrowed, and tilled so that under the discipline of cultivation it may bear fruit from seed. "Therefore the Lord God sent him (Adam) to till the ground from which he was taken": "the field" (Gn. 3:23,18). There, man was to learn that the bearing of fruit may be effortless in a garden but not in a field. "The field is the world" (Mt.13:38). Man in the field must not only obey and keep the Seed of the Lord's command, but he must also be subjected to suffering before he can bear fruit. The tree of a garden bears fruit year after year and continues to flourish after each gathering, but not the crop of a field, since the plant bearing the full grain in the ear withers and dies when its fruit is reaped.

Thus, while he is in the field of the world, Man suffers and dies until the day he may return once more to the joys of life everlasting in that Garden called Paradise.

**3. Sons of my Threshing.** The expression: "0 my threshing, and the son (ben) of my threshing floor, that which I have heard from the Lord of Hosts, the God of Israel, I have declared (nagad-'to set forth plainly') to you," is found in Isaiah (21:10) and contains hidden wisdom. For just as the ground of a field has to undergo the tribulation of being plowed, harrowed, and tilled before it can bear the fruit of the full ear of grain from the seed sown in it, so does the ear of grain itself have to undergo the trial of being reaped, threshed, winnowed, brayed, ground, kneaded, pressed, and baked before it finally becomes bread. And since the wheat or children seeds within the ear of grain are brought forth from the husks through the painful threshing on the threshing floor, they may be said to be "sons" of the great threshing floor, just as the fruit-ears of grain may be said to be "sons (bennim) of the field" (Job 5:23 Literal translation). Having been tried through the tribulation of the threshing-for "what does he know who has not been tried?" (Sir. 34:9, Latin Vulgate [LV])-the "son" of the threshing floor is ready to hear and understand what the prophet will declare to him.

*4.* **Bread of Man.** In the Garden of Eden, Man did not have to produce his own food, the Lord provided for him out of the herbs, seeds, and fruits of His creation (Gn. 1:11, 29; 2:8-9, 16). But when Man was exiled into the field, he had to labor in sorrow for nourishment and make his own food: "bread." And because Man has to suffer before he can eat the "bread of men" (Ezek. 24:17, 22; Gn. 3:19), Man's bread is referred to as "the bread of affliction" (1 Kgs. 22:27; 2 Chr. 18:25; Dt. 16:3), "bread of sorrows" (Ps. 127:2), and "bread of adversity" (Is. 30:20) for it is "bread gotten by sweat" (Sir. 34:26, [LV]). It may be easy for the ground of a garden to "bring forth" a fruit tree, and for Man to pluck and eat its fruit, but the ground of a field must be worked upon before it can "make (asah) fruit" (Lev. 25:19, 21; 2 Kgs. 19:30; Is. 37:31) from seed.

And because its soil is "the earth whose fruits are raised by labor" (Test. of Issachar 5:5), Man in the field has to plow, harrow, sow, till, reap, thresh, winnow, bray, grind, sift, knead, mould, and bake before he can eat the bread he has made.

But God is good, for when Man has worked in the field "to the exhaustion of his strength" (Sir. 31:4 Hebrew text), the Lord in turn makes the ground "yield . . . her strength" (Gn. 4:12) to him. And from the "bread (lechem) out of the earth" (Ps. 104:14) Man receives his strength back, being nourished by that "bread which strengthens man's heart" (Ps. 104:15; 1 Sm. 28:22) and "comforts" (Jgs. 19:58) him.

A garden is for fruit trees, and a field for grain. We know that if Adam had kept the Seed of God's command in the Garden of Eden, he would have in a certain way, become a Treeman bearing the fruit of the knowledge of God. By the same token, Man in the field of exile, is finally expected to be a Breadman becoming himself "the bread of understanding" (Sir. 15:3) if he keeps the seed of God's Word. Life was pleasant for Man in the Garden of Eden, but in the field of exile, Man has to undergo the same travail that the ground of a field is subjected to, in order to be able to produce good fruit. Thus, in the field: "Man is land suffering" (Epistle of Barnabas 6:9), because "his fruitful field both soul and body" (Is. 10:18), can only be fruitful through labor and suffering (Gn. 3:16, 17, 19; 41:52). Man in the field can consider his own "back as the ground" (Is. 51:23)and say as King David did: "Upon my back have the plowers plowed and made their furrows long" (Ps. 129:3).

Knowing that in his field of exile Earthman is meant to become a Breadman, we can see why Joseph dreamt of himself and his family as sheaves of grain (Gn. 37:6-8) and why people are referred to as "bread" (Nm. 14:9; Ps. 14:4; 53:4). After all, when Jesus Messiah came to share our life in the field of exile, was He not born in the little town called "the house of bread" (Bethlehem) and placed in a grain bin (Lk. 2:12,16)? And did He not have to suffer and die (Mt. 16:21; Mk. 8:31; 9:12; Lk. 9:22; 17:25; 24:26-27; Acts 3:18; 17:3; Heb. 2:10; 5:8-9; Is. 52:13; 53:12; Zech. 12:10; 13:7) so that He could give Himself to us a "True Bread," the "Living Bread" who is our "Bread of Life" (Jn. 6:32, 48, 51; Mt. 26:26; Mk. 14:22; Lk. 22:19; 1 Cor. 10:16; 11:23)? If a good man is "like a tree planted by streams of water that yields his fruit in his season" and in the same Psalm "the wicked . . . are like chaff which the wind drives away" (Ps. 1:3-4), are not the righteous as grains of wheat? Rightly did the Rabbis say: "the righteous, all of them are as wheat fit for storage" (Midrash Song of Songs Rabbah 7.3) and "Israel is like a heap of wheat" (Pesikta Rabbati, Piska 10.3; Shoher Tob 2.12; Midrash Numbers Rabbah 1.2; Midrash on Psalms 2.13, 14). In the day the Lord shall "put . . . in the sickle for the harvest is ripe" (Jl. 3:13), the just shall be gathered as wheat, but "the wicked . . . are as stubble before the wind, and as chaff that the storm carries away" (Job 21:17, 18; Ex. 15:7; Pss. 35:5; 83:13; Is. 5:24; 17:13; 29:5; 40:24; 41:15-16; Jer. 13:24; (Gn. 37:6-8) Hos. 13:3; Na. 1:10; Mt. 3:12). But let us take heart for the book of job tells us that if we are good: "you shall come to your grave in ripe old age, as a shock of grain comes in, in his season" (Job 5:26). The "wise" are "like ripe ears of grain" said the Rabbis (Sotah 5a; Bechoroth 58a, [BT]) and "kiss the wheat" (Bar = either "wheat" or "son") was interpreted by them to mean: "kiss the Messiah" (Rabbis David Kimchi and Solomon Jarchi on Ps. 2:12.

See also Midrash on Psalms 2.13).

If we search the field of rabbinic writings we shall find that there is a Jewish tradition about a Suffering Messiah (see Targum Jonathan on Is. 53:4-6; Ibn Ezra on Zech. 13:7; Pesikta Rabbati, Piska 36.1-2; 37.1; 34.2; 31.1; Midrash Ruth Rabbah 5.6 re Is. 53:5; Midrash Tanchuma 7.53; Sanhedrin 98b; Sukka 51b-52a and Baraithas, [BT]; Siphre to Lev. 12:10 re 5:17; Yalkut Shimoni, Sect. 125, 415, 469; R. Moses Haddarshan on Gn. 1:3 re Is. 53:7; Zohar Vol. 11.212; R. Abrabanel, R. Alsheh, R. Eliyya de Vida, R. Eleazar ben Kalir re Is. 52:13-53:12. See also Testament of Benjamin 3:8).

Man in the field was not only likened to grains of wheat or bread, but also to "dough" (Midrash Genesis Rabbah 14.1; 17.8; 34.10; Tanchuma on Gn. 1.28; 3.53; Tanchuma Noah 1; Mezora 9; Berakoth 17a, [BT], Ibid. 7d, Jer. T; Shabbath 31b-32a, [BT], Ibid. 2.5; Jer. T. Tosephta Kiddushin 5.2; Yalkut to Prov. 962; Siphre to Dt. 45; Rabbi Abahu on Gn. 6:6; Philo, De Sacr. Abel et Cain, 107, 108). As St. Paul said: "Purge out the old leaven, that you may be a new dough" (1 Cor. 5:7) for truly "we many are one Bread" (1 Cor. 10:17). And since ideally in the Garden of Eden Man was to be himself the fruitful garden of the Lord, so is Man in the field expected to be as the Lord's own rich field of grain. "May he be as a flourishing field of grain," said the Rabbis concerning the Messiah (Ps. 72:16 in the Midrash Genesis Rabbah 48.10; 86.1; Midrash Ecclesiastes Rabbah 1.9). Thus the prophet Hosea addresses the people as a field and exhorts them "Sow to yourselves in righteousness" (Hos. 10:12). "Sow then for yourselves good things in your soul that you may find them in your life" (Test. of Levi 13:6).

If we consider the two basic goals set for Earthman, namely, that he was to be as a Treeman bearing the fruit of the knowledge of God if he had kept the Seed of God's command while in the Garden; and now potentially a Breadman becoming himself "the bread of understanding" (Sir. 15:3) if he keeps the Seed of God's Word in the field. We shall then understand why these two concepts are often found side by side in Holy Scripture (Ps. 1:3-4; Job 13:25; 24:20, 24; Is. 5:24; Mal. 4:1; Mt. 3:10, 12; Lk. 3:9, 17). And we shall also grasp why it took a "tree" (ets) to make bitter water "sweet" (Ex. 15:23-25) and "flour" (qemach) to make bitter fruit palatable (2 Kgs. 4:39-41). Were not the enemies of Jeremiah given insight when they said of him: "Let us destroy the tree with the bread (lechem) thereof" (Jer. 11:19, Literal translation)? Or why did the Rabbis say that "the fruit of the tree of knowledge was wheat" (Midrash Genesis Rabbah 15.7; Berakoth 40a, [BT])? Of course they were mistaken for it takes labor and suffering to bring forth wheat and there was no sorrow in the Garden of Eden, but perhaps they were speaking in a hidden sense of the ideal Man full of knowledge from the fruit of knowledge and full of understanding from the bread of understanding.

Man in the Garden of Eden could have through obedience alone pleasantly brought forth the fruit of knowledge found hidden within the Seed of God's command. But in the field of exile, he must "labor to know" (4 Ezr. 5:34, 37), and as a disobedient child be reproved and "come to knowledge by the scourge of God" (2 Mc. 9:11), and learn through "the chastisements of knowledge"(I Q S 3:1, Dead Sea Scrolls; Pss. 119:71; 94:12) that when one does not obey a simple command, he shall be taught obedience through suffering. The ancients knew that "pain brings forth perception" (Philo, De Leg. Alleg. 111.216) and "suffering leads to knowledge" (Herodotus 1.207; Aeschylus, Ag. 176f., 249f.; Sophocles, Oed. Col. 1.1-7; Corpus Hermeticum 1.4ff., 482; Irenaeus 1.4; 11.4-5; V.4; Plotinus, Enn. IV.7-8). As the book of Proverbs says: "a rod is for the back of him who is void of understanding" (10:13) for "the rod and reproof give Wisdom" (29:15).

In the "great trial of affliction" and suffering that he undergoes in his field of exile, Man shall "abound in . . . faith and utterance, and knowledge" (2 Cor. 2:7; Eph. 6:19-20; Col. 4:3), and "he shall see the travail of his soul and be satisfied by his knowledge . . ." (Is. 53:11), but only after he has undergone the same travail the ground of a field is subjected to before it bears the crop of grain. "Happy is the man whom God corrects, therefore despise not the chastening of the Almighty for . . . you shall know . . . you shall know and . . . you shall come to your grave in ripe old age, as a shock of grain" (Job 5:17, 24, 25, 26). For "what does he know who has not been tried?" (Sir. 34:9, LV). "He that has not been tried, knows little" (Sir. 34:10, Greek Sinaiticus text). So well-known was the relationship between suffering and knowledge that when the Alexandrian Jewish scribes translated the Hebrew text that said: "the misery of Man (*adam*) is great upon him" (Eccl. 8:6) they rendered it in Greek: "the knowledge (*gnosis*) of Man is great to him" (Eccl. 8:6 Septuagint). And in the Hebrew text where it was said of the Lord that "He made him (Jacob) to *understand*" (Dt. 32:10), they rendered it in Greek: "He *chastised* him" (Dt. 32:10

Septuagint). The Romans also knew this, for when they in turn translated the Greek text that said: "To whom has the *understanding* of Wisdom been made manifest?" (Sir. 1:7, Greek Mss. 23, 55, 70, 106, 253), they rendered it in Latin: "To whom has the *discipline* of Wisdom been made manifest?" (Sir. 1:7, Vetus Latina and Vulgate texts). It was common knowledge that: "whosoever loves chastisement (*musar*) loves knowledge, but he that hates reproofs is brutish" (Prv.12:1), he is "brutish in his knowledge" (Jer. 10:14; 51:17) and "has not the understanding of a Man" (Prv. 30:12). "They have beaten me and I know not" (Prv. 23:35) said the foolish man, because "a fool though scourged does not understand" (Prv. 17:10 Greek text) but "the godly man . . . makes his sufferings contribute to the increase of his knowledge" (*Corpus Hermeticum, Libellus IX. 4b*). Thus the book of Wisdom says of the people of God that "when they were tried . . . being disciplined in mercy, they knew . . ." (11:9) for had not Moses told the people: "The Lord your God led you these forty years in the wilderness to humble you and to prove you . . . he humbled you and suffered you to hunger . . . that he might make you know . . ."? (Dt. 8:2, 3). Knowing this "he who has knowledge will not complain when he is disciplined" (Sir. 10:25 Greek text) for he knows that it is through "the discipline of Wisdom" (Sir. 1:7, LV) that he shall obtain His knowledge in the field. "No chastening for the present seems to be joyous but grievous, nevertheless, afterward it yields the peaceful fruit of righteousness to those who have been trained by it" (Heb. 12:11). "Who will set scourges over my thoughts and the discipline of Wisdom over my heart that they spare me not for my lack of knowledge?" (Sir. 23:2 Greek text, Literal translation). "0 Lord . . . we pray before You that You would give us Seed to our heart and cultivation to our understanding so that there may come fruit from it" (4 Ezra 8:6).

"Man is born to labor" (Job 5:7) and "all his days are sorrows and his labor grief" (Eccl. 2:23). "Afflictions . . . you yourselves know that this is to be our lot" (1 Thess. 3:3)-in His field. For just as "Jacob was perfected as the result of discipline" (Philo, De Agr. 42) so are we to bring "fruit to perfection" (Lk. 8:14) through the discipline of suffering. Day by day as we labor for Him to "make (poeio) fruit a hundredfold" (Lk. 8:8), we shall understand that we are "made perfect through sufferings" (Heb. 2:10; 5:8, 9). "Teach me . . . that I may produce fruits" (Odes of Sol. 14:7). What He shall teach us in the field, is that just as the child is "father" to the full grown man, so "the father of knowledge (as a fruit) is the Word of Knowledge" as a Seed (Odes of Sol. 7:7), but we must keep that Seed of His Word if we desire to receive the fruit of knowledge from it.

God is kind, and He did a wonderful thing to comfort us in our grievous labors: He hid His Wisdom, Understanding and Knowledge in the Seeds of His commands. There is great Wisdom, Understanding, and Knowledge hidden within the Seed of His Word; we have only to keep and do His commandments and these treasures will be open to us. For thus says the Lord: "Keep therefore the Words of this Covenant and do them so that you may understand" (*sakal*); "Observe to do all that is written (in the Law) . . . for then you shall make your way prosperous and, you shall have understanding" (*sakal*); "he that keeps the Law gets the understanding thereof"; "Behold, I have taught you statutes and judgments, keep therefore and do them for this is your wisdom and understanding in the sight of the nations" (Dt. 29:9; Jos. 1:7, 8; Sir. 21:11; Dt. 4:5, 6). That is why the Law is called: "the Law of life and good understanding" (Sir. 45:5 Hebrew text), and also why the Psalmist cried out: "I have more understanding than all my teachers because I keep Thy precepts" for "through Thy precepts I get understanding" (Ps. 119:100, 104). Thus it was said of King Hezekiah that he "kept the commandments which the Lord commanded Moses, and the Lord was with him and he understood" (*sakal*), for indeed, "a good understanding have all those who do His commands" (2 Kgs. 18:6, 7; Ps. 111:10).

In keeping the Seed of His Word and doing His commands we shall understand that in the names "Ephrathah" (*fruitful*) and Bethlehem (*house of bread*) are hidden the two stages of mankind. And we shall know that it was only fitting that He should choose to be born there, who came down from heaven to be "the First-fruit" (1 Cor. 15:23) and "Living Bread" (Jn. 6:51) of Man.

# IV
# EPILOGUE

They came weeks later who saw the star and followed it. Men of the night who came from the gate of the dawn, bringing with them gifts of gold, and frankincense, and myrrh for the child.

And when they found him with his mother in a little house not far from the inn,

They fell down and worshipped him.

They left as suddenly as they had come, and no one saw them depart except my wide-eyed brother ox.

I remember now . . . it is the simple who find Him first, because they have Wonder for their guide.

Wise men follow a slower star.

We are in Egypt in a small village not far from the banks of the Nile.

Here have we lived for the past two years.

O "Egypt . . . so well watered everywhere like the Garden of the Lord" (Gn. 13:10).

"Out of Egypt have I called My Son" (Hos. 11:1; Mt. 2:15)-back to the field where He was taken from.

I know that we shall soon commence the long trek back to the land of His birth.

For it must be there that He is to become the Bread of Man.

It is past midnight and I see the horns of the heavenly ox pointing towards the East to guide us.

The carpenter comes with my halter and the blanket he shall lay upon me;

Following close behind him is the mother and her Child.

We are ready now . . .

She has just placed Him in front of her upon my back.

He leans forward, and I feel His little hands tugging at my ears.

# BIBLIOGRAPHY

*Hebrew Bible*

Kahle, P. Prolegomena to Kittel's Biblia Hebraica. Leipzig,1937.

Kittel, R. Biblia Hebraica, 3d ed. Leipzig, 1937.

*Greek Bible (Septuagint)*

Rahlf, A., ed. Septuaginta. 2 vols. Stuttgart, 1935.

Swete, H. B., ed. The Old Testament in Greek. 3 vols. Cambridge, 1909-1922.

*Latin Bible (Latin Vulgate, LV)*

Biblia Sacra. (Ed. Facultatis Theologiae Parisiensiset Seminarii Sancti Sulpitii). Rome, 1947.

Hertzenauer, P. M., ed. Biblia Sacra Vulgatae. Rome,1914.

*The Book of Wisdom*

Deane, W. J., ed. The Book of Wisdom. Oxford, 1881.

Goodrick, A. T. S., ed. The Book of Wisdom. London, 1913.

Gregg, J. A. F. The Wisdom of Solomon. Cambridge, 1909.

Grimm, C. L. W., ed. Das Buch der Weisheit Leipzig, 1860.

Reider, J. The Book of Wisdom. New York, 1957.

Winston, D. The Wisdom of Solomon. Garden City, NY, 1979.

Ziegler, J., ed. Sapientia Salomonia. (Septuaginta vol. XII, 1), Gottingen, 1962.

*Sirach (Ecclesiasticus)*

Hart, J. H. A., ed. Ecclesiasticus-The Greek Text of Codex 248. Cambridge, 1909.

Levi, I., ed. The Hebrew Text of the Book of Ecclesiasticus. Leiden, 1969.

Oesterley, W. O. E., ed. Ecclesiasticus. Cambridge, 1912.

Peters, N., ed. Das Buch Jesus Sirach. Freiburg, 1956.

Segal, M. S. Sefer Ben Sira ha-Shalem. [Hebrew]. Jerusalem, 1959.

Smend, R., ed. Die Weisheit des Jesus Sirach. Berlin, 1906.

Ziegler, J., ed. Sapientia lesu Filii Sirach. (Septuaginta vol. XII, 2). Gottingen, 1965.

*The Book of Maccabees*

Abel, F. M. Les Livres des Maccabees. Paris, 1949.

Bissell, E. C., ed. The First and Second Books of Maccabees. New York, 1880.

Fairweather, W. and Sutherland, J., eds. The First Book of Maccabees. Cambridge.

Hadas, M., ed. The Third and Fourth Books of Maccabees. New York, 1953.

Starcky, J., ed. Translated by F. M. Abel. Les Livres des Maccabees. Paris, 1961.

*Pseudoepigrapha*

Baars, W., ed. The Psalms of Solomon. Leiden, 1972.

Bate, H. N. The Jewish Sybylline Oracles.New York, 1918.

Bernard, J. H., ed. The Odes of Solomon. Cambridge, 1912.

Bogaert, P., ed. L'Apocalypse Syriaque de Baruch. 2 vols. Paris, 1960.

Box, G. H. II Esdras (IV Ezra). London, 1917. Charles, R. H., ed. The Apocrypha and Pseudoepigrapha of the Old Testament. 2 vols. Oxford, 1913.
--The Apocalypse of Baruch. (2 Baruch). Oxford, 1896.
--The Book of Enoch, 2d ed. Oxford, 1912.
--The Book of the Secrets of Enoch. (2 Enoch). Oxford, 1896.
--The Book of Jubilees. Oxford, 1908.
--The Testaments of the Twelve Patriarchs with Greek, Armenian and Slavonic Variants. Oxford, 1908.
--Fragments of a Zadokite Work. Oxford, 1912.

Charlesworth, J. H., ed. The Odes of Solomon. Oxford,1973.

Dejonge, M., ed. The Testaments of the Twelve Patriarchs.Assen, 1953.
--Testamenta XII Patriarchum. [Greek text]. Leiden, 1964.

Gray, G. B. The Psalms of Solomon. Oxford, 1913.

Harris, J. R., ed. The Psalms of Solomon. Cambridge, 1909.

Harris, J. R. and Mingana, A., eds. The Odes and Psalms of Solomon. 2 vols. Manchester, 1916/1920.
Holm-Nielsen, S., ed. Die Psalmen Salomos. Guttersloh, 1977.

Klijn, A. F. J., ed. Die Syrische Baruch-Apokalypse. Tubingen, 1976.

Kmosko, M., ed. Apocalypsis Baruch. (Patrologia Syriaca 1:2, Cols. 1056-1207.) Paris, 1926.

Knibb, M. A. and Ullendorff, E., eds. Ethiopic Book of Enoch: New Edition in the Light of the Aramaic Dead Sea Fragments. 2 vols. Oxford, 1978.

Malan, S.C. The Book of Adam and Eve. Edinburgh, 1882.

Morfill, W. R. The Book of the Secrets of Enoch. Oxford, 1896.

Myers, J. M. I and II Esdras. Garden City, NY, 1974.

Oesterley, W. O. E. II Esdras. London, 1933.

Picard, J. C., ed. Apocalypsis Baruch Graece. Leiden, 1967.

Ryle, H. E. and James, M. R., ed. and trans. Psalms of Solomon. Cambridge, 1891.

Rzach, A. Oracula Sibyllina. Leipzig, 1891.

Schodde, G. H., ed. The Book of Jubilees. Oberlin, Ohio, 1888.

Stone, M. E., ed. Testament of Levi. [English translation of the Armenian Text]. Jerusalem, 1969.

--The Armenian Version of 4 Ezra. (University of Pennsylvania Armenian Text and Studies I). Missoula, 1979.

Swete, H. B., ed. The Psalms of Solomon [G reek Text] with the Greek Fragments of the Book of Enoch. Cambridge, 1899.

Terry, M. S., trans. The Sibylline Oracles. 2d ed. London. 1899.

Vaillant, A. Le Livre des Secrets d'Henoch. (2 Henoch). Paris, 1952.

### *Dead Sea Scrolls*

Brownlee, W. H. The Dead Sea Manual of Discipline. (IQS). New Haven, 1951.

Burrows, M. and Trever, J. C., eds. The Dead Sea Scrolls of St. Mark's Monastery. 2 vols. New Haven, 1950-1951.

Davies, P. R., ed. I Q M: The War Scroll from Qumran. Rome, 1977.

Dupont-Sommer, A., ed. The Essene Writings from Qumran. Oxford, 1961.

Holm-Neilson, S. Hodayot: Psalms from Qumran. (Thanks giving Hymns Scroll-I Q H). Aarhus, Denmark, 1960.

Jongelin, B. Le Rouleau de la Guerre des Manuscrits de Qumran. Assen, 1962.

Leaney, A. R. C. The Rule of Qumran and Its Meaning. (I Q S, Community Rule). Philadelphia, 1966.

Licht, J. The Thanksgiving Scroll. [Hebrew.] Jerusalem, 1957.

Lohse, E. Die Texte aus Qumran. Munich, 1964.

Mansoon, M., ed. The Thanksgiving Hymns.(I Q H). Leiden, 1961.

Rabin, E., ed. The Zadokite Documents. [Cairo Damascus Document-CD]. Oxford, 1954.

Schechter, S. Fragments of a Zadokite Work. Cambridge, 1910.

Sukenik, E. L. Osar hammegiloth Haggezanoth. [Hebrew Text of I Q H and Fragments]. Jerusalem, 1954-1957.

Van der Ploege, J. Le Rouleau de la Guerre. (War Scroll-I Q M). Leiden, 1959.

Wernberg-Moeller, P. The Manual of Discipline.

(Community Rule-I Q S). Leiden, 1957.

Yadin, Y., ed.The Scroll of the War of the Sons of Light Against the Sons of Darkness. (War Scroll-I Q M). Jerusalem, 1956.

***The Targums of the Old Testament***

Etheridge, J. W. The Targums of Onkelos and Jonathan Ben Uzziel on the Pentateuch with the Fragments of the Jerusalem Targum from the Chaldee. London, 1862. Repr. Ktav, NY,1968.

Sperber, A., ed. The Bible in Aramaic. 4 vols. London, 1959.

Stenning, J. F. The Targum of Isaiah. Oxford, 1949.

***Ancient Middle Eastern, Greek and Latin Texts***

Boeckh, A., ed. Corpus Inscriptionum Graecarum. 4 vols. Berlin, 1877.
--Corpus Inscriptionum Latinarum. 14 vols. Berlin, 1863.
--Corpus Inscriptionum Semiticarum. Paris, 1881.

Driver, G. R. Canaanite Myths and Legends. (Old Testament Studies 3). Edinburgh, 1956.

Ginsberg, H. L. The Legend of King Keret (BASOR Supplement 2-3). New Haven, 1946.

Gordon, C. H. Ugaritic Handbook. (Analecta Orientalia XXV). Rome, 1947.
--Ugaritic Manual. (Analecta Orientalia XXXV). Rome, 1955.
--Ugaritic Textbook. (Analecta Orientalia XXXVIII). Rome, 1965.

Gray, J. The Keret Text in the Literature of Ras Shamra. 2d ed. Leiden, 1964.

Knudtzon, J. A., ed. Die-El-Amarna Tafeln. Voderasiatische Bibliothek. Leipzig, 1907-1916. Mercer, S. A. B. The Tell-El-Amarna Tablets. 2 vols. Toronto, 1939.

Peiser, L., trans. Translation of the Lachish Tablet. (Orientalische Literatur-Zeitung, Jan. 1899). Berlin.

Torczyner, H. The Lachish Letters. Jerusalem, 1938.

Virolleaud, La Legende de Keret. Paris, 1936.

Whitehouse, 0. C. The Cuneiform Inscriptions and the Old Testament. 2 vols. London, 1888.

### *Talmuds*

1) *Jerusalem*
Behrend, B. Z. Talmud Yerushalmi. [Hebrew]. Posen, 1866.
Schwab, M., ed. Le Talmud de Jerusalem. 6 vols. Paris, 1960.
(Repr. of 1878 edition.)

2) *Babylonian*
Talmud Babli. [Hebrew]. Wilno, 1927.

Epstein, I. and Cohen, A., ed. and trans. The Talmud Babli with the Minor Tractates. 18 vols. and 2 vols. London, 1961 and 1965.

### *Midrash (Rabbah)*

Midrash Shemoth Rabba. Wilno, 1887.
Freedman, H. and Simon, M., ed. and trans. The Midrash. 10 vols. London, 1961. Hallevy, E. E., ed. Midrash Rabbah. 8 vols. Tel Aviv,1965.

### *Midrashim*

Braude, W. G., trans. Midrash on Psalms. 2 vols. New Haven, 1959.
Buber, S., ed. Midrash Haggadol Rabbah. Wilno, 1887.

--Midrash Debarim Rabbah Zutta. Vienna, 1885.
--Midrash Mishle. Wilno, 1893.
--Midrash Samuel. Wilno, 1924.
--Midrash Tanchumah. 4 vols. Wilno, 1885.
--Midrash Tehillim. Trier, 1892.

Grunhut, L., ed. Sepher haLikkutim. Jerusalem, 1898 1902.

Jellinek A., ed. Midrash Konen. (In Beth haMidrash Vol. II, pp. 23-29). Leipzig, 1853-1877. --*Sepher Noah.* (In Beth haMidrash Vol. III, pp. 155-160). Leipzig, 1853-1877.

Kalisch, I., ed. Sepher Yetzira. New York, 1877.

Kohen, Eliyahu ha, Midrash Talpiyot, Warsaw, 1875.

Lauterbach, J. Z., ed. and trans. Mekilta de Rabbi Ishmael, 3 vols. Philadelphia, 1933-1935.

Margolioth, M. Midrash Haggadol on Genesis. Jerusalem, 1947.
--Midrash Haggadol on Exodus. Jerusalem, 1956.

Noah, M. M. Book of Dasher. New York, 1840. Padua, A. M. Midrash Lekah Tob on Genesis, Exodus, Numbers, and Deuteronomy. Wilno, 1880.

Rabinowitz, E. N. Midrash Haggadol on Leviticus. New York, 1932.

Rosenthal, L. A. Sepher ha Yashar. Berlin, 1898.

Schechter, S., ed. Midrash Haggadol. Cambridge, 1902.

Midrash Haneelam (In the book of Zohar, folio 13b). See Zohar.

### *Midrashim Collectanea*

Braude, W. G. and Kapstein, I. J., eds. Tanna debe Eliyyahu. Philadelphia, 1981.

Eisenstein,J.E.,ed.Ozar Midrashim. 2 vols.Jerusalem, 1914.

Ginsberg, L., ed. The Legends of the Jews. 6 vols. Philadelphia, 1968.

Jellinek, A., ed. Beth ha Midrash. 6 vols. Leipzig, 1853-1877.

### *Pesikta*

Braude, W. G., ed. and trans. Pesikta Rabbati. New Haven, 1965.

Braude, W. G. and Kapstein, I. J., eds. Pesikta de Rab Kahana. Philadelphia, 1975.

Buber, S., ed. Pesikta de Rab Kahana. Lyck, 1868.
--Pesikta Zutrathi. Lyck, 1868.

Friedmann, M. Pesikta Rabbati. Vienna, 1880.

### *Pirkei*

Friedlander, W. G., ed. Pirke de Rabbi Eliezer. New York, 1965.

Goldin, J., ed. Pirke Aboth de Rabbi Nathan. New Haven, 1965.

Hertz, J. H., trans. Sayings of the Fathers (Pirke Aboth). New York, 1945.

Higger, M., ed. Pirke Rabbi Eliezer. Jerusalem, 1948.

Schechter, S. Aboth de Rabbi Nathan. Vienna 1887.

### *Siphre*

Friedmann, M. Siphre to Numbers and Deuteronomy. Vienna, 1864.
Horowitz, H. S. and Rabin, I. A. Siphre on Numbers and Siphre Zutta. Leipzig, 1917.
--Siphre on Deuteronomy. Berlin, 1939.
Weiss, J. H. Sifra Torath Kohanim (On Leviticus). Vienna, 1862.

***Tanchumah (Yelammedenu)***

Buber, S. Tanchumah. 4 vols. Wilno, 1885. --Yelammedenu. (In Sepher ha Likkutim I, 2a-20a). See Midrashim.

***Toledoth***

Hyman, A. Toledoth Tannaim weAmoraim. 3 vols. London, 1910.

Vries, B. de. Toledoth haHalakah haTalmudit. TelAviv, 1962.

Weinberg, J. Toledoth ha Targumin. New York, 1954.

***Torah Shelemah***

Kasher, M. M., ed. Torah Shelemah. 28 vols. Jerusalem, 1927-1977ff.

***Yalkut***

Buber, S., ed. Yalkut Makiri. 2 vols. Berdyczew, 1899.

Epstein, A., ed. Yalkut Shimeoni. Wilno, 1898. --Yalkut to Proverbs. (In Yalkut Shimenoi Sect. 929-965).
--Yalkut to Zechariah. (In Yalkut Shimeoni Sect. 596-609).

King, E. G. TheYalkut on Zechariah. Cambridge, 1882.

***Zohar***

*Zohar Chadash. (On Canticles). Livorno, 1866.*

*Margolioth, M., ed. Zohar: With Commentaries.*

*[Hebrew]. 3 vols. Jerusalem, 1964. Margolis, R., ed. Zohar. [Hebrew]. 3 vols. Jerusalem, 1840-1846.*

*Sperling, H. and Simon, M., ed. and trans. The Zohar. London, 1933.*

***Philo Judaeus***

*Colson, F. H., Whitaker, G. H., and Marcus R., trans. Philo. 12 vols. (Loeb Classical Library). London, 1929-*

*1953.*

***Josephus***

*Thackeray, H. St. J. and Marcus, R. Josephus. 9 vols. (Loeb Classical Library). London, 1971.*

***Ancient Greek Writers***

*1) Aeschylus*
*Dronke, G. Die Religiosen and Sittlichen Vorstellungen des Aeschylus and Sophocles. Leipzig, 1861.*

*Weir Smyth, H. Aeschylus. 2 vols. (Loeb Classical Library). London.*

*2) Herodotus*
*Godley, A. D., trans. Herodotus. 4 vols. (Loeb Classical Library). London, 1920-1925.*

*3) Plotinus*
*Armstrong, A. H. Plotinus. 6 vols. (Loeb Classical Library). Cambridge, MA, 1966.*

*4) Sophocles*

*Campbell, L. Sophocles. London, 1879.*

*Storr, F. Sophocles. 2 vols. (Loeb Classical Library). London, 1928-1939*

***Hermetica***

*Nock, A. D. and Festugiere, M., eds. Corpus Hermeticum. Paris, 1945-1954.*
*Scott, W., ed. Hermetica: The Ancient Greek and Latin Writings which contain religious and Philosophical Teachings attributed to Hermes Trime gistus. 3 vols. Oxford, 1924-26.*

***Ancient Christian Writers***

*1) The Apostolic Fathers*

*Grant, R. M. and Graham, H. H., eds. The Apostolic Fathers: Vol II-First and Second Clement. New York, 1965.*

*Kleist, J. A. Epistle of Barnabas. Westminster, MD, 1948.*

*Kraft, R. A. The Apostolic Fathers: Vol. III*

*Barnabas and the Didache. New York, 1965.*

*Lake, K., ed. The Apostolic Fathers. 2 vols. Cam bridge, MA, 1946.*

*Lightfoot, J. B. and Harner, J. The Apostolic Fathers. 2 vols. New York, 1891.*

*2) Diognetus*

*Radford, L. B., ed. The Epistle to Diognetus. London, 1908.*

*3) Ephrem*

*Asemani, J. S., ed. Bibliotheca Orientalis: Vol. IEphrem. Rome, 1728.*

*4) Eusebius of Caesarea*

*Bardy, G., ed. Eusebe de Cesaree: Histoire Ecclesiastique. 3 vols. (Sources Chretiennes, 31, 41, 55). Paris, 1952-1958.*

*Mras, K., ed. Praeparatio Evangelica of Eusebius. Paris, 1954-1956.*

*Klosterman, I., ed. Eusebius of Caesarea: Onomastikon. Paris, 1904.*

*5) Irenaeus*

*Roberts, A. and Donaldson, J., trans. AnteNicene Fathers: Vol. 1-Irenaeus, pp. 315578. Grand Rapids, 1975.Robinson, J. A., ed. Irenaeus: Demonstration of the Apostolic Preaching. London, 1920.*

*6) Jerome*

*Lagarde, P. de, ed. Hieronymi: Quaestiones Hebraicae inLibro Geneseos. Leipzig, 1868.*

## *Holy Land Guides*

*Adler, M. N., trans. and comm. The Itinerary of Benjamin of Tudela. London, 1907.*

*Meistermann, B. New Guide to the Holy Land. London, 1923.*